GROUND COVER PLANTS

JOHN NEGUS

GW00492953

HarperCollins*Publishers*

Editors Maggie Daykin, Susanne Mitchell
Designer Chris Walker
Production Controller Craig Chubb
Picture research Moira McIlroy

First published 1989 by
HarperCollins Publishers

This edition published 1992

© Marshall Cavendish Limited 1989, 1992

A CIP catalogue record for this book is available from the British Library.

Photoset by Litho Link Ltd., Welshpool, Powys, Wales
Printed and bound in Hong Kong by Dai Nippon Printing Company

Front cover: Helianthemum nummularium 'Old Gold'
Back cover: Garden Scene
Both photographs by Michael Warren

CONTENTS

INTRODUCTION

In the wild, plants grow together in a wonderful mixture of flowers and foliage to cover meadow, hedgerow and woodland. Whether it's cow parsley or buttercup, bluebells or primroses, there are ground-hugging plants for every place. Garden plants are equally accommodating and one way to make gardening easier is to grow a range of easy-care spreading shrubs, perennials or grasses. These, used either alone or in groups, will provide a carpet of weed-suppressing leaves and flowers.

Choice candidates Wherever you garden, whether on chalk, peat, heavy clay or sand, in woodland shade, full sun, by the sea or on an exposed hillside, there are plants you can rely upon to blanket the soil.

Mat-forming carpeters such as periwinkle and ivy enjoy probing deep shade. Some root as they spread. Others are sprawlers, such as *Rosmarinus lavendulaceus* and *Ceanothus thyrsiflorus repens*, which enliven many a sun-drenched patio or steep bank.

Many herbaceous plants are efficient weed suppressors. Thicket-forming, strap-leaved day lilies colour summer days with gold, pink or bronze trumpet-shaped blooms, and they will thrive in either well-drained or marshy soil.

Geraniums (cranesbill) are specially adaptable: *G. macrorrhizum*, a rooting spreader that has broad aromatic leaves and sprays of deep magenta flowers in 'Bevan's Variety', colonizes heavy shade. So does *G.* 'Russell Prichard', its finely cut leaves and short stems decked with magenta-pink flowers. It is so eager to please, that it not only forms a weed-proof blanket around trees and shrubs but forages in the deepest shade beneath them.

Hosta, another herbaceous plant, is virtuous indeed and prized for its rosettes of beautiful heart- and lance-shaped leaves in many striking hues, and spikes of lily-like lilac, white or amethyst flowers in summer. Enjoying full sun or shade – where its leaves are larger and

LEFT Hostas are among the most untemperamental of plants and actually flourish in shade. Watch out for slugs though; they love the tender young leaves.

TOP RIGHT A sunburst of golden *Milium effusum* 'Aureum' is a lovely sight in a mixed border.

RIGHT Silvery pale *Luzula sylvatica* is another very attractive slender grass suitable as ground cover.

more impressive – it remains fresh and vigorous in light, parched soil and is equally unconcerned when immersed for weeks in a rain-flooded border.

Another able carpeter for light, moisture-starved soil is pernettya, whose clusters of bright polystyrene-textured violet, magenta or white

berries seem to glow with inner light on dark November days.

Another berried sprawler is *Cotoneaster* 'Skogholm Coral Beauty', whose small, evergreen leaves are brightened by orange-red autumn fruits.

Conifers, specially prostrate varieties of *Juniperus horizontalis,* such as 'Blue Chip', whose flat feathery fans have a silvery blue tint in summer, and 'Prince of Wales', with bright green leaves, are ideal partners for heathers and taller conifers.

Ferns are marvellous for colonizing cool, damp, shady spots unloved by many other plants. Particularly striking are the creeping, hardy maidenhair, sensitive, ostrich, lady and polypodium species.

Climbers need not necessarily ascend. Honeysuckle, climbing hydrangea and Virginia creeper, are equally happy prostrating themselves over paving or borders.

Alpine sprawlers, such as golden alyssum, aubrieta and saxifrages are enchanting whether spilling over rock outcrops or clothing clefts. Apart from shade-loving Bowles' golden grass (*Milium effusum* 'Aureum') and *Luzula maxima* 'Marginata', with its arresting white-rimmed leaves, most grasses are avid sun worshippers.

Do find room also for tussocky blue-green *Festuca glauca* and imposing *Stipa calamagrostis,* enjoyed for its fountains of feathery plumes.

Be warned though. Some plants are rampageously invasive. The gold and green-flecked dead nettle, *Lamiastrum galeobdolan* 'Variegatum' is one of them. Relegate this intruder to a hedge bottom or beneath a shade-casting tree where its enthusiastic take-over bid will be tempered by poor light.

SOILS AND PLANTING

If you meet a plant's soil needs, you will be more than halfway there to encouraging its happy establishment. But don't fight Nature. If, for example, your soil is chalky it makes little sense to grow acid-soil lovers, such as rhododendrons, heathers and pernettyas. Whatever soil you have – loam, clay, sand, stones, chalk, peat or bog – seek out plants that avidly enjoy it.

Loam The ideal soil. A nicely balanced and nourishing mix of clay and sand that warms quickly in spring. It is usefully water retentive but drains freely, so roots are never waterlogged. It is neither too acid nor too alkaline – so you will find that most plants excel in it.

Clay soil Notoriously difficult but not insurmountable. Late, cold and badly drained – puddles form quickly after rain – it is sticky and greasy when wet and shrinks, cracks and becomes rock-hard when dry.

Condition it by applying lime, which converts it into crumbs, thus

Potentilla fruticosa revels in chalky soil, flowering prolifically. Here, 'Yellow Queen' gives of her best.

RIGHT The rock rose, *Helianthemum nummularium,* is another chalk-lover. It also comes in many colours.

BELOW RIGHT Dainty dianthus new hybrids are at home in quick-draining, dryish soil.

improving drainage and air flow. Improve its texture, too, by forking in plenty of well-rotted organic matter: old manure, spent mushroom compost (valued for its lime content), peat, pulverized bark and garden compost. Coarse grit, sharp sand or lumpy wood ash are good clay 'splitters'.

Disregarding its inhospitality are such shrubby plants as *Potentilla fruticosa,* ivies, berberis, hypericum, snowberry, and impressive herbaceous plants – crocosmia, rodgersia and polemonium.

Stony soil Warmer and easier to condition than clay, so growth is earlier. Poor humus-deficient and sharply draining stony or sandy soils should be fortified with moisture-conserving organics such as peat, well rotted manure and garden compost.

Plants that don't mind these soils are artemisias, anthemis, eryngiums and the other 'silvers', and *Geranium sanguineum,* alpine phlox, bergenia and pernettya.

Chalky soil Limy soils are prone to drying out. They are also impoverished because chlorophyll-essential foods such as iron, manganese and phosphates are less available in highly alkaline conditions. This results in stunted, yellow-hued leaves. Fortify porous chalk with organic manures, peat, 'Forest Bark' Ground and Composted Bark and garden compost.

Plants that enjoy a high degree of chalk are clematis, viburnum, *Potentilla fruticosa,* helianthemum, dianthus and thyme.

9

RIGHT Tightly packed small flowerheads of *Azalea* 'Mother's Day' growing well in an acid soil.

BELOW RIGHT *Epimedium rubrum's* young leaves are tinged with ruby red and even more spectacular in the autumn, when they turn to orange and yellow. The tiny flowers, produced in May, are pink. Another plant for acid soil.

Acid soil Acid, peaty soils have many virtues. Usually well endowed with moisture-conserving humus, they are enjoyed by a wide range of plants. Their balance from acid to alkaline is fairly easily adjusted by adding lime. If marshy, drain them by means of a herringbone system of land drains leading to a ditch or soakaway.

Rhododendrons, azaleas, heathers, Himalayan poppies, ferns and epimediums are among the many plants that enjoy this type of soil.

Marshy spots Use them to advantage; boggy, poorly-aerated soil is a haven for moisture-loving plants. Eager kinds are rodgersias, marsh marigolds, day lilies, candelabra primulas, plumy-flowered astilbes, *Euphorbia palustris*, the carpeting willows and *Geranium pratense*.

10

Planting techniques Separate invasive spreaders, such as pachysandra, periwinkle and *Rubus calycinoides* which – if left to 'collide' – become a tangled mess, by interspersing them with clump-forming 'buffers' that grow more slowly. Good ones are hosta, cotoneaster, potentilla and santolina. Group most plants in threes, fives or sevens; never plant them singly.

Prepare the soil for planting by forking deeply, adding 'Forest Bark' Ground and Composted Bark or well-rotted manure and 113g per m^2 (4oz per sq yd) of bone meal.

When setting out a containerized plant, remove it carefully from its pot, gently tease out some of the outer, fine feeding roots from the compacted mass and nestle the root ball into the hole at the same depth as it was in the pot. Pack moist peat around its roots and refill the hole with soil. Firm as you go. Use your hands if the plant is small or the heel of your boot if it is large.

Finally, prick over the soil to remove compacted footprints and water well to settle soil around the roots before mulching with a 5cm (2in) layer of peat or old manure.

Planting a steep bank Prevent soil from washing away by first covering the bank with fine mesh netting, making a hole just sufficiently large to enable you to plant through it and then pegging it down around the root system.

Alternatively, construct a series of steps with firmly positioned logs, layering soil behind them. Then plant in the terraces thus created.

Stepped banks make an ideal site for massed small ground cover plants, and these will keep the soil in its place as well as being a delight to the eye.

SHADE BRIGHTENERS

Yes, there is a fine range of architectural and flowering plants, ready and able to colonize light and densely shaded areas. No, you can't plant them in unprepared soil. Under trees and shrubs, carpeters are competing with food and moisture-sucking roots. Shadowy sites between buildings can be desiccating wind tunnels and plants to colonize them must have a rugged constitution, and a little help from you.

LEFT Equally at home in a wild garden or a shady border, *Tellima grandiflora* grows to about 60cm (2ft) and bears its bell-shaped flowers from April to June. The purple-leaved *T.g.* 'Purpurea' is not so effective in shade.

RIGHT Hardy, bushy *Hebe pinguifolia* 'Pagei' withstands icy blasts and the small grey-green leaves lighten a gloomy spot even when the May to June flowers are long gone.

Damp, dappled shadows There are many spreading, ground-hugging herbaceous kinds for moist, lightly shaded positions. Choice among them are finger-leaved helle-bores, specially the orientalis hybrids with their saucer-shaped blooms in rich plum shades; and dead nettles *(Lamium maculatum)* such as 'Shell Pink', 'White Nancy' and 'Beacon Silver', prized for their creamy or silver-suffused leaves. Another winner is *Brunnera macrophylla,* a rapid spreader with big, broad, heart-shaped leaves and enchanting sprays of sky-blue forget-me-not-like flowers.

Find room, too, for the ornate hosta family, lily-of-the-valley (convallaria). Or plant varieties of bugle (ajuga) with a choice of rounded green, wavy-edged leaves in 'Jungle Beauty', rose-magenta and cream in 'Burgundy Glow' and burnished purple in 'Purpurea', all with short spikes of tubular, bright gentian-blue flowers in spring.

Primroses love moist spots where sunlight shafts between branches. Other prime candidates are fox-gloves, ferny-leaved ladies' lockets (dicentra), and *Tellima grandiflora,* with bright green leaves – bur-nished in winter – and small upright

12

Plants you can rely upon to form weed-stifling canopies are *Alchemilla mollis,* with its delightful, frothy sprays of sulphur-yellow flowers; bergenia in its vivid rose-red 'Abendglut', pinkish white 'Snow Queen' and pure white 'Silberlicht' forms, the latter a gem with large glossy evergreen leaves, often copper tinted in winter; and epimedium, whose small marbled leaves provide a foil for exquisite, miniature columbine-like flowers in yellow, red or terracotta that appear in spring.

Others that thrive in spite of arid conditions are coral-belled heuchera, *Viola labradorica* – a welcome bronzy-green-leaved invader with pale blue flowers that forever self-seeds in the most inhospitable places – and the aromatic-leaved *Geranium macrorrhizum,* in its magenta and soft lilac varieties.

sprays of creamy bells. A glade of Solomon's seal, its glossy, oval leaves on arching stems set with serried rows of waxen, creamy tubular blooms, is unforgettable.

A wealth of ferns also enjoy this situation, developing extra large fronds when lightly shaded. Spectacular are *Matteuccia struthiopteris,* like a tall shuttlecock, and *Blechnum tabulare,* with large, leathery evergreen fronds.

For drier spots You can establish many a good-hearted spreader or sprawler among a network of moisture-hungry tree roots. But first you must take out substantial planting holes, ideally 60cm (2ft) square and deep. Fill them with plenty of nourishing, moisture-conserving old manure or well-rotted garden compost, or peat or pulverized bark laced with a liberal sprinkling of blood, fish and bone meal or fish meal.

Shade from buildings The cruel effect of keen, whipping winds must be considered when planning for shade lovers to cheer gloomy gaps between houses. Shrubs which don't mind icy blasts are evergreen cotoneasters, such as *C. humifusus,* with tiny leaves and red berries, *C.* 'Skogholm Coral Beauty', an intrepid sprawler with orange fruits, and deciduous *C. horizontalis,* whose fishbone arrangement of stems shine with a bounty of small, scarlet berries in autumn and early winter. Birds love them.

Equally adaptable, are evergreen, dense and hemispherical *Berberis candidula* and its faster growing 'Amstelveen' variety, both of which have silvery undersides to their glossy leaves. Another is *Hebe pinguifolia* 'Pagei', a hardy, bushy shrub whose wide mats of small blue leaves are a blaze of tiny spikes of pearl-white flowers in summer.

13

IN PLACE OF GRASS

A lawn is a fine but demanding feature. It needs regular mowing, feeding, keeping free of weeds and many other attentions. In shady areas, grass may be reluctant to grow at all. Steep banks are awkward and hazardous to cut, and an embarrassment when the grass is long and weedy. Patches between paving slabs are tedious to edge round. Fortunately, there is a solution: such areas are readily carpeted with colourful, labour-saving ground-cover plants.

Grass substitutes In light soil in full sun, small lawns are effectively replaced with a spreading carpet of chamomile (*Anthemis nobilis*), which forms a filigree of rich green leaves if you use the non-flowering 'Treneague' variety.

Another grassy-leaved evergreen is liriope, its short but commanding spikes of lavender-purple flowers in autumn making a fine 'lawn' in full sun or light shade. It also tolerates dryish soil. More intriguing, is purplish-black, strap-leaved *Ophiopogon planiscarpus* 'Nigrescens', whose slender leaves form a grass-like mat.

In poorly lit, north-facing areas – close to or under trees or near buildings – where even shade-tolerant lawn grasses are reluctant to establish, Bowles' golden grass (*Milium effusum* 'Aureum') makes a pool of soft, sunny yellow in spring and early summer.

Ivies are superb for carpeting lightly shaded or sunny dells. Plant them closely to thickly interweave. Choose from the varieties of *Hedera helix* – 'Glacier', with small silver-grey leaves; dark green 'Gylmii', 'Green Survival', 'Hibernica' or 'Pin Oak' are my recommendations.

Bank notes Steep slopes, impossible to mow and prone to weeds, are easily draped and stabilized with spreaders that set down roots wherever their stems touch the soil.

Evergreen periwinkles (vinca) excel in this role. Happy in the sun or shade, *V. minor* 'Aurea' with golden leaves and white flowers, 'Bowles' Blue', with large blue blossoms, and 'Alba' – with white flowers which shine like stars in shadowy spots – colonize rapidly.

All ivies grip the soil. The larger, golden-variegated *Hedera colchica* 'Dentata Variegata' or similar 'Paddy's Pride', will soon form a golden variegated cloak. Sinuous, evergreen and rapid carpeting, *Rubus calycinoides* – an ornamental blackberry – has appealing dark green puckered leaves, white felted

beneath, but its white summer flowers are insignificant. The queen of the dense canopy formers must be rose of Sharon *(Hypericum calcynum)* an evergreen with large, saucer-shaped, yellow blooms from June to September.

Pocket these Gaps in crazy paving are happy homes for bright candidates whose roots revel in cool soil beneath the slabs.

Sprawling, summer-flowering sun rose (helianthemum), in its 'Wisley Pink', 'Wisley Primrose', 'Double Cream' or 'Yellow with Orange Eye' varieties, never ceases to please. Tussocky, richly clove-scented dianthus thrive in these conditions, too. Double, creamy white 'Mrs Sinkins' and green-eyed single white 'Musgrave's White' have a certain old-fashioned appeal.

LEFT Pale-leaved mixed ivies spill down a bank; an unusual and effective grass substitute.

ABOVE For a colourful carpet, try the brilliant and bounteous *Campanula* 'Stella'.

Other gap-filling mat formers are the red and white daisy-flowered *Anacyclus depressus; Acaena* 'Blue Haze' with reddish stemmed, bluish bronzy leaves and brownish flowers; and *Sagina pilifera* 'Aurea', golden to lime-green mossy cushions decked with tiny white flowers. *Artemisia schmidtiana* 'Nana' is an enchanting filigree of silver-blue leaves; and *Campanula* 'Stella' is so bounteous that its stems are almost hidden beneath starry blue flowers.

Others you can rely on to form a pleasing embrace and round off sharp paving slabs are *Ajuga reptans* in its 'Bruaherz' variety, in which purplish-bronze leaves contrast with tiny, deep blue flowers; *Arenaria montana*, small leaved and a foam of white blossom from spring to summer; and alpine phlox, such as *P. subulata* 'White Delight', and the vivid rosy-red 'Temiscaming'.

Blue flowers are always welcome and you certainly won't regret planting *Veronica prostrata* in its 'Loddon Blue' and 'Blue Sheen' varieties. Vigorous trailers, both are massed with sky-blue spikes of bloom in spring and summer.

Brighter hedge bottoms These are frequently dry, impoverished and colonized by coarse weeds. Fortify the soil with organic manure and plant such winning drought resisters as woodruff *(Asperula odorata)*, a dense spreader with short, fetching stems of whorled leaves and starry white flowers in spring; or *Brunnera macrophylla*, a perennial forget-me-not with big, hairy heart-shaped leaves and peeping, spring blue flowers. *Geranium sanguineum*, with 'dove's foot' leaves and magenta-red flowers, and 'Lancastriense' with white, pink or lavender-blue flowers are also ideal.

15

AFTERCARE

Having established your chosen carpeters in well-prepared soil, speed them along by mulching with bulky, moisture-conserving organic manures and feed them regularly with a balanced fertilizer. Keep in check any weeds, pests and diseases, too.

LEFT When applying weedkiller, always use a sprinkler bar and, even then, protect nearby plants from the spray. Don't spray if there's any wind.

BELOW Two useful sprinklers designed for watering: one rotary and the other oscillating.

Weeding If you planted through a perforated breathable membrane which keeps the root area cool and moist, allowing air, water and plant food to percolate to the roots, but checks weed growth, you should not be troubled with fast-growing annual weeds such as chickweed, groundsel and shepherd's purse.

If a membrane wasn't used, and new plantings are having to compete with seedling weeds, 'Weedol' is called for. Apply it accurately with a small sprinklebar attached to a watering can, or an ICI weedkiller applicator, taking care not to splash cultivated plants as you work.

Watering Each day, in an average garden in spring and summer, hundreds of gallons of moisture are 'pulled' from the soil by trees, shrubs and border plants and a further amount is lost to the atmosphere.

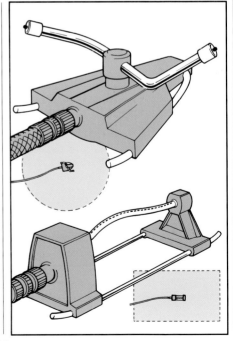

RIGHT A good mulch helps to conserve moisture, once applied – and will suppress all but the most determined of weeds.

BELOW A soak or seep hose is covered in small perforations so once you have turned on the water supply you can leave the hose to do the rest for you.

Mulching After watering, conserve moisture by covering the surface with 5-7.5cm (2-3in) of peat, pulverized 'Forest Bark' Ground and Composted Bark or 'Forest Bark' Chipped Bark. All of these will suppress weeds, too.

Pruning The shrubs I have mentioned do not require pruning in the accepted sense. Simply trim them when they begin to get leggy, to keep them shapely. Do this in spring and early summer, ideally after flowering. Heathers should also be trimmed – using shears – when flowers fade.

Ground-cover roses also appreciate a spring prune. Shorten extra long and awkward shoots, to keep them from becoming unsightly and encourage both branching and a well-furnished base.

Remove spent blooms from herbaceous and alpine plants and cut back dead fern fronds in early spring.

If dry, windy weather follows shrub pruning, water the cuts daily to keep bark moist and encourage strong new shoots to form.

If geraniums, bergenias, brunnera, epimediums, lily of the valley, tellima and asperula – shade lovers all and usually planted in the rooty soil beneath trees and shrubs – are to make good progress, it is vital to keep their roots cool and moist. Achieve this by watering copiously in dry weather; ideally you should be using a seep hose which has multiple perforations.

Propagation Shrubs, herbaceous and alpine plants that root as they spread are easily increased by slicing off rooted portions with a spade and replanting them in autumn or spring.

The non-rooting, hummocky or sprawling shrubs are easily propagated from half-ripe heeled cuttings in late July or early August. Simply tug a side shoot from the main stem, pare back the tag of bark to within 3mm (⅛in) of the base and remove lower leaves. Then dip the base in hormone rooting powder and insert cuttings to half their length around the edge of a 7.5-10cm (3-4in) half-pot of gritty compost. Root in a shaded cold frame. Mist cuttings regularly to keep them perky or cover pots with perforated plastic bags.

Clematis are best increased in July from 6.5-7.5cm (2½-3in) long, internodal cuttings. These are stem sections, cut between joints (nodes) at the base and to just above two buds and two leaves at the top. Root them like shrub cuttings.

You can also propagate clematis

Woolly aphids at work.

and other climbers from layers. Choose a low shoot, and make a 2.5cm (1in) sloping cut into the middle of a joint; keep it open with a small stone or sharp sand. Dust with hormone rooting powder such as 'Keriroot', peg the cut section into gritty soil and keep it damp. Tie the tip of the shoot to a cane.

The tussock-forming herbaceous plants, such as festuca, hemerocallis, astilbe and aruncus are divided into well-rooted portions with a spade. This can be done in early autumn or early spring.

PEST ALERT

Aphids (greenfly, blackfly) These minute, winged creatures cluster thickly around fleshy shoot tips of roses, euonymus and many other plants. Control with primicarb-based 'Rapid', which kills within 30 minutes but does not harm beneficial bees, ladybirds and lacewings.

Slugs These actively chew fleshy leaves and stems on warm, wet nights. Eradicate with metaldehyde-based ICI Mini Blue Slug Pellets,

Leaf miner labyrinth.

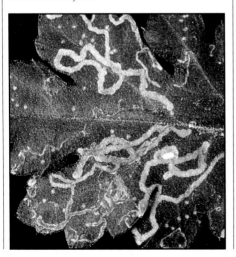

which are unattractive to pets, and less visible to birds.

Caterpillars Sure signs of these pests are leaves holed and chewed. Spray with 'Picket', containing permethrin, or with 'Bug Gun' for Roses and Flowers, based on pyrethrum.

Rose leaf-rolling sawfly Leaves become tightly tubed, with grubs hidden inside. Pick off and burn affected foliage and spray the plant with 'Picket' or 'Sybol', containing pirimiphos-methyl.

Leaf miner A pest of honeysuckle and some other plants, producing a labyrinth of 'mines' between upper and lower leaf surfaces. Control with 'Picket' or 'Sybol'.

Woolly aphid Sticky, fluffy white colonies cluster around stems of cotoneaster and other shrubs. Spray the infestations very forcefully with 'Rapid' or 'Sybol'.

Mealy bug attack.

Rose powdery mildew.

Brown scale Limpet-like scales suck sap from young cotoneaster shoots. Spray with 'Sybol' in late summer.

Mealy bug Fluffy white colonies of aphid-like creatures cluster around leaf joints. Spray forcefully with 'Sybol' as soon as you see them.

DISEASES

Rose powdery mildew Signs are white-matted leaves and shoots, and stunted growth. Control with Benlate + 'Activex'; this contains benomyl, which also controls black spot disease; 'Nimrod'-T based on bupirimate and triforine, which also eradicates black spot and rust, or 'Roseclear', based on bupirimate, triforine and pirimicarb, which effectively controls black spot, rust and aphids, too.

Rose rust Orange pustules on leaf undersides later turn black. Apply 'Nimrod'-T or 'Roseclear' at 14-day intervals from early spring to mid summer.

Rose blackspot Circular, purple-black spots on leaves and stems; leaves fall early. Tackle with 'Nimrod'-T or 'Roseclear'.

PLANT ASSOCIATIONS

The art of creating a memorable, weed-excluding tapestry of relatively maintenance-free flowers and foliage, is to select plants with comparable needs. They should also be of similar vigour, to avoid one plant dominating another. Whether you wish to clothe gaps in paving, cloak the soil between trees or shrubs, furnish a dry and sunny – or cool, damp – spot, drape a steep bank, rockery or salty, wind-blasted seaside garden, there is a pot pourri of plants to serve you.

Some lateral thinking here has produced a splendid substitute for wistaria to highlight a wooden bridge: *Alchemilla mollis* with its froth of sulphur-yellow flowers and attractive foliage. Try it at the foot of a trellis.

Fringe benefits Border edges are special, and low-growing arrangements that brightly billow and sprawl are worth getting right.

Try grouping creamy white and green-striped Yorkshire fog grass *Holcus mollis* 'Variegatus', red-belled *Heuchera* 'Coral Cloud' and *Artemisia stelleriana,* whose finely cut, silver-grey leaves are highlighted by yellow, mimosa-like flowers in summer. *Ajuga reptans* 'Brauherz' (a mat of purple-bronzy leaves and deep blue flower spikes), *Arabis ferdinandii coburgii* 'Old Gold', prized for its golden-variegated leaves, and *Artemisia schmidtiana* 'Nana', which yields low filigree mounds of silver-grey foliage, are a stunning association. So, too, are *Veronica teucrium* 'Shirley Blue's brilliant azure flower spikes embraced by a carpet of golden marjoram *(Origanum vulgare* 'Aureum') or a waterfall of *Alchemilla mollis'* frothy yellow flower sprays backed by *Hosta* 'Thomas Hogg' with its rosettes of green, creamy-edged, heart-shaped foliage; a winning combination.

In twilight shade Weed-infested patches around trees and shrubs will not occur if you underplant with leathery-leaved, white-flowered bergenias, Bowles' golden grass, flecked, silvery-leaved *Pulmonaria saccharata* 'Argentea' and white-belled Solomon's Seal. Alternatively, interplant thrusting, sword-leaved *Iris foetidissima* (drought-tolerant, with biscuit-yellow flowers followed by fat seed pods which split to reveal varnished orange seeds) with *Hosta sieboldiana,* which is valued for its massive, crimped, blue-green leaves and spikes of white, lily-like flowers, and *Blechnum tabulare,* a tall and elegant ladder fern.

Some geraniums romp in shade. Specially good are white-flowered *G. macrorrhizum* 'Album' or *G.* 'Russell Prichard', entwined with red-flowered *Epimedium macranthum* 'Roseum' and ferny-leaved, bright scarlet-flowered *Dicentra eximea* 'Luxuriant'.

A fine combination is bright silvery-pink *Geranium endressii,* which flowers most of summer, set to romp and carpet beneath the golden foliage of those small trees, *Robinia pseudoacacia* 'Frisia' and *Gleditsia triacanthos* 'Sunburst'.

Around the house For hot spots, create a cool cloak of silver-blue and white with the foliage of *Ruta graveolens* 'Jackman's Blue', *Stachys lanata* 'Silver Carpet', silver-white *Artemisia* 'Powis Castle', *Festuca glauca* – a tufted blue grass – and Cineraria 'Silver Dust', a short-lived perennial best raised from seed each year. Heighten interest with the deep purple-blue flowers and silvery-grey leaves of *Lavandula spica* 'Hidcote'.

ABOVE RIGHT Lots of cool colours in this mixed planting for a terrace in hot sun.

RIGHT So many low, mat-forming plants look good together that the only problem is dwindling down the choice.

The aptly named poached egg plant, *Limnanthes douglasii* is a winner in any yellow and white theme. It also has a slightly scented flower and is a firm favourite with our friends, the bees.

A sunny-yellow and white theme would be the poached egg plant *(Limnanthes douglasii)* with *Dianthus* 'White Ladies' or 'Mrs Sinkins', yellow-flowered *Hypericum olympicum* and *Cerastium tomentosum,* a trailing carpeter with starry white blooms.

Cool, north-facing borders are home to fragrant white-flowered lily-of-the-valley *(Convallaria majalis),* scarlet-flowered cranesbill *(Geranium sanguineum),* and, respectively, its white and pink forms, 'Album' and 'Lancastriense'. Combine all four; the effect will please you.

Another way to transform a chilly spot is to drape it with hardy evergreen shrubs and climbers, such as, respectively, *Cotoneaster* 'Skogholm Coral Beauty' and small, silver-leaved *Hedera helix* 'Glacier' or its larger, suffused gold and green-leaved relation, *H. colchica* 'Paddy's Pride' for really rapid growth.

Patio plantings Increase the appeal of that sunny paved area by leaving a few strategically placed gaps for interplanting with golden-flowered *Alyssum saxatile* 'Citrinum', double-white *Arabis caucasica* 'Plena' and creamy pink-leaved, blue-flowered *Ajuga reptans,* 'Burgundy Glow'.

Alternatively, group golden-variegated-leaved *Euonymus fortunei* 'Emerald 'n' Gold' with *Hebe pagei* 'Pinguifolia', to create a gold and silver-blue mat.

With their roots in cool, moist soil beneath paving slabs, thymes revel in baking warmth above. Brush your hand over a patchwork quilt of red-flowered *Thymus serpyllum* 'Coccineus', white 'Albus' and speckled gold-leaved 'Doone Valley' and enjoy their spicy aroma.

Sedum spathulifolium 'Cappa blanca' has fleshy, creamy-grey rosettes and small starry yellow flowers that contrast stirringly with the purple-red leaves and densely packed pink flowers of *S. spurium* 'Purple Carpet'.

Spreading conifers and heathers look superb spilling over the edge of a patio. Enliven yours with *Picea pungens* 'Hoopsii', a dwarf Colorado spruce with small, broad, silvery-blue needles, embraced by carpeting, golden-leaved *Erica carnea* 'Foxhollow'.

Steep sunny banks are hazardous to mow but easily transformed and stabilized with soil-hugging carpeters. There are many colourful choices. For instance, the newish race of ground-cover roses, pioneered by Mattocks of Oxford, are ideal. Try an association of single or semi-double white 'Partridge' which has glossy, disease-resistant foliage, with deep rose-pink 'Pheasant' and double pale pink 'Pink Drift'. They will flower from July to August.

Alternatively, group 'Rosy Cushion' with its semi-double, ivory-white and rose-pink flowers, with large single pink 'Smarty', whose blooms are borne in large trusses on arching branches, and 'Red Blanket', which has semi-double rose-red flowers and dense glossy leaves that hold well into winter.

Yet another fine display is achieved by interplanting the rose varieties 'White Bells', 'Pink Bells' – with soft pink fully double blooms – and 'Red Bells'. All have a similar habit of growth and sprawl over the soil to form a 60cm (2ft) carpet.

If your soil is thin and sandy and tends to parch in dry spells, plant evergreen, drought-defying sun roses (helianthemum), in bloom from May to July. Large-flowered white 'Wisley White', yellow 'Wisley Primrose', double yellow 'Jubilee' and flame-orange 'Firedragon' are all good choices.

Euonymus fortunei 'Emerald 'n' Gold' provides living proof that you need not always rely on flowering plants for variegated colour. This characteristic also makes it a perfect partner for silver-green foliage, with which a uniform gold would not do at all.

Climbers are splendid for draping a bank. Evergreen *Clematis armandii's* stems, decked with large three-lobed leaves and skeins of vanilla-scented white flowers in spring, romp thickly over a warm site. Interweave it with the evergreen honeysuckle, *Lonicera japonica* 'Halliana', prized for its sweetly scented, biscuit-yellow flowers in summer.

Heathers also create dense, spreading and tussocky mats. Summer-flowering *Erica cinerea*, *E. tetralix*, *E. vagans*, *Daboecia cantabrica* and *Calluna vulgaris* need an acid soil, while winter-flowering *Erica carnea* and that wide-spreading hybrid, *E.* × *darlyensis*, tolerate a little lime.

Year-round colour is easily won. Brighten winter with *Erica carnea* 'Springwood White', *E. carnea* 'Springwood Pink' and *E.* × *darleyensis* 'Ghost Hills', enjoyed for its pink flowers and cream-tipped new shoots. Cheer the summer months with *E. cinerea* 'Purple Beauty' and *E. tetralix* 'Pink Star'.

Light up late summer and autumn with *E. vagans* 'Cream', *Calluna vulgaris* 'White Lawn', 'Golden Carpet', a superb foliage variety whose summer gold leaves assume orange and red tints in winter, and *Daboecia cantabrica* 'Rosea', with suffused-pink, white flowers.

For marshy spots In nature, poorly drained wetlands are habitats for an amazing range of choice plants. In gardens, boggy patches are happily colonized by some of our more flamboyant species.

Candelabra primulas, whose blooms are borne in whorls (tiers) around the stem, are very appealing. Primula 'Bressingham Strain' sports pink, salmon or orange blooms with contrasting eyes. Then there's orange

LEFT For a group of varied, mat-forming plants, you need look no further than heathers and heaths. Furthermore, they provide colour in the garden in deepest winter, and do so with the minimum of care.

RIGHT, ABOVE The leaves of rodgersia afford wide-spread cover, while the tall flower spikes give you something to look up to.

P. *bulleyana*, purple *P. burmanica*, crimson *P. pulverulenta* and yellow *P. helodoxa*. Interplant with plumy-flowered astilbes, such as white 'Snowdrift', scarlet 'Fanal' and rosy-red 'Federsee'.

Alternatively, combine candelabra primulas with globe flowers (trollius) – 'Canary Bird' is lemon-yellow, 'Fireglobe' is deep orange and 'May Gold' is golden-yellow.

An association of astilbes and ostrich feather fern *(Matteuccia struthiopteris)*, with its unfurling, upright fronds resembling elegant shuttlecocks, is memorable.

Other arresting displays are easily devized with statuesque foliage plants. Try grouping *Rodgersia tabularis*, with its dinner-plate leaves poised centrally on fleshy stems, or *R. pinnata* 'Elegans', whose broad fingered leaves foil big,

creamy, astilbe-like blooms, with *Ligularia clivorum* 'Desdemona' whose large rounded, purplish leaves offset large sprays of chrome-yellow flowers in late summer.

Alternatively, team *Rheum palmatum* 'Atrosangineum' which forms a weed-surpressing mound of 90cm (3ft) wide leaves, dark green on top, rosy-purple beneath, with *Ligularia stenocephala* 'The Rocket', which has rounded, deeply cut leaves and long narrow cones of black-stemmed, yellow flowers.

Rock garden drapes With a little ingenuity it is possible to clothe outcrops, pockets and fissures with accommodating and colourful mat formers to greatly reduce the chore of weeding.

Brighten spring with an inter-planting of dense sprawlers – aubrietas, such as deep violet 'Dr Mules', reddish-purple 'Bob Saunders' or light pink 'Bressingham Pink' – white iberis 'Snowflake', a shrubby, small-leaved evergreen; and primrose-yellow *Alyssum saxatile* 'Citrinum' or its 'Dudley Neville Variegated' form with buff-yellow flowers and striking silver-mottled leaves.

For a summer display, group starry, light-blue-flowered campanula 'Stella' with *Hypericum reptans*, a mass of large yellow blooms, and white-flowered *Nierembergia rivularis*. All are determined carpeters.

There are many spreading rock garden conifers. The prostrate noble fir *(Abies procera* 'Glauca Prostrata') with silver-blue, bottlebrush stems, and rich reddish flower cones in spring, contrasts happily with golden-leaved *Erica carnea* 'Foxhollow', *Thymus* 'Anderson's Gold' or the grey-white *Sedum spathulifolium* 'Cappa blanca'.

25

Alpine geraniums are valuable weed smotherers. Small, pink-flowered, glossy-leaved, *G. dalmaticum* associates endearingly with the starry gentian-blue blossom of *Lithospermum diffusum* 'Heavenly Blue' – which must have a lime-free soil – and the eager spreading alpine phlox, *Phlox subulata* 'White Delight'.

Enrich late summer with *Polygonum vaccinifolium*'s massed display of small pink pokers, which rise from a blanket of tiny leaves.

Houseleeks (sempervivums) are perfect for filling rocky fissures and spreading a weed-proof mantle over and around outcrops.

Seaside gardens Give ground-covering candidates every chance to establish by enriching poor sandy soil with humus-forming organic manures and fertilizers.

Screen them from the salt-laden winds by planting a shelter belt of sycamore, hawthorn, *Quercus ilex* or varieties of whitebeam *(Sorbus aria)*, 'Majestica', for example.

Arrange a bright, shrubby display with an interweave of evergreens such as *Cotoneaster* 'Skogholm Coral Beauty', adorned with bright orange autumn fruits; *C. conspicuus decorus*, which quickly forms a dense mound of dark green leaves, grey and woolly beneath; Mexican orange *(Choisya ternata)* with citrus-scented, white flowers in spring and autumn, and rose of Sharon *(Hypericum calycinum)*, whose zestful carpeting stems are tipped from June to September with large yellow blooms with shaving brush centres.

Alternatively, create a zone of silver by interplanting cotton lavender *(Santolina chamaecyparissus)* with *Senecio maritima*, whose stems and leaf undersides are coated with white down. Bright yellow daisy flowers appear in summer.

There is also a fine selection of resilient herbaceous plants that shrug their leaves at salty spray. Group *Achillea millefolium* 'Moonshine', with silver-filigreed leaf-clad stems topped with plate-like, bright

Silvery grey-green foliage creates a nice change of mood in the garden and provides a perfect foil for many bolder colours as well as merging well with its own kind. Here, *Santolina chamaecyparissus* displays its lemon-yellow July flowers. Keep the flower colour in mind when planning the overall scheme.

Butterflies will hover and glide all summer long if you plant even the smallest of thyme lawns. Here, *Thymus drucei* forms a pretty, resilient carpet that will spring back with no harm done. The flowers appear from June to August.

yellow flowers in June and again in autumn; *Crocosmia masonorum,* with its thrusting sword leaves and upright to arching fiery orange and scarlet flower cones in late summer; *Crambe maritima,* with waved and waxen blue-green leaves and short stems of creamy white flowers in early summer; and *Polygonum bistorta* 'Superbum' with cyclamen-pink pokers.

Butterfly flowers Choice herbaceous carpeters for sunny borders, with nectar-rich flowers that lure tortoiseshell, peacock, red admiral, painted lady and other butterflies, are mushroom-headed achilleas, such as *A. millefolium* 'Lilac Beauty', a superior yarrow; *Thymus serpyllum* varieties, among them 'Pink Chintz' and crimson 'Coccineus'; and *Sedum spectabile* 'Brilliant', whose bright mauve-pink flowers make good landing stages.

For rock gardens, there's maiden pink *(Dianthus deltoides),* with starry, carmine flowers that sprout from mats of dense green leaves – it associates well with thyme – and thrift (armeria) 'Dusseldorf Pride' with light wine-red heads on 13cm (5in) stems in midsummer.

Blooms for bees Invaluable pollinators – essential for a good set of fruit and runner beans – bees should be encouraged by planting nectar- and pollen-rich flowers.

Plant a tempting association of such shrubs as *Cotoneaster humifusus,* whose white-flowering, red-berried shoots root as they spread; *Berberis thunbergii,* with suffused-red, straw-yellow flowers followed by bright red fruits – birds love them – and creeping blue blossom *(Ceanothus thyrsiflorus* 'Repens').

27

CHOICE CARPETERS

Cloaking the ground with a fetching mantle of weed-suppressing leaves or flowers, there are dozens of able contenders – shrubs, conifers, climbers, herbaceous, rock plants, grasses, ferns and annuals among them – to help us garden easily and effortlessly. Once established, their low-maintenance carpets have an undeniable and enduring appeal.

Evergreen azaleas

Derived mainly from tiny-leaved *Rhododendron kiusianum*, it's the undemanding Glendale, Gable, Japanese Large Flowered and Kurume Hybrids – a confection of blossom from April to June – which reward us well. Choice kinds are low, rounded and bushy, magenta-purple 'Hatsugiri', vermilion-orange 'Addy Wery', rich terracotta 'Bungonishiki', pink 'Hinomayo' and white 'Niagra'. Slow growing, they thrive in ordinary, well-drained, lime-free soil, but are best in damp, shady spots away from chilly winds. Ht 60cm-90cm (2-3ft). Sp 100-120cm (34-48in). No regular pruning required.

Berberis

Clusters of orange or yellow bell-like spring flowers, golden, pink or purple foliage, fiery autumn tints and bounteous autumn berries. There are deciduous and evergreen kinds. The fast-suckering clumps will form impenetrable thickets. Deciduous *B. thunbergii* 'Green Carpet', ht 1m, sp 1.5m (3 × 5ft), has light green leaves which turn bronzy red before falling in autumn; *B. wilsonae*, of similar size, is dense and spreading with coral-red berries.

A choice hummock-forming evergreen is *B. candidula* 'Telstar', ht 60cm, sp 120cm (24 × 48in), and semi-evergreen *B. media* 'Parkjuweel', ht 80cm, sp 90cm (36in) has almost spineless leaves which assume sunset tints in autumn. All thrive in ordinary to poor, well-drained soil and full sun. Thin and trim after flowering.

Ceanothus thyrsiflorus 'Repens'

Rapid colonizer. A dense evergreen commonly called creeping blue blossom, its exploring small-leaved shoots are smothered with mid-blue flowers in spring. Ideal for a sunny, well-drained bank. Ht 1m. Sp 3m (3 × 10ft). No pruning.

Prolifically flowering, pink 'Hinomayo'; an evergreen azalea

Cotoneaster
Multitude of slender stems clad with small, rounded leaves and tiny pink-budded, June-white flowers. Red or orange berries in autumn. Finest of the prostrate evergreen carpeters are *C.* 'Skogholm Coral Beauty', ht 30cm, sp 240cm (12 × 96in); *C. humifusus (dammeri),* spreading at around 60cm (2ft) a year, and *C. h.* 'Oakwood', similar but more compact in form.

Deciduous and much larger, the fish-bone cotoneaster *(C. horizontalis),* ht 50cm, sp 150cm (20 × 60in), provides a dazzling display of scarlet berries and fiery autumn leaf tints. Well-drained soil, any aspect, full sun or light shade. No pruning.

Cotoneaster horizontalis

Euonymus fortunei (radicans)
Evergreen, hardy and covering the soil with a dense mat of small, brightly-hued leaves. Choose from 'Silver Queen', ht 40cm, sp 100cm (16 × 40in), with white and green leaves that turn rosy pink in winter; 'Emerald 'n' Gold', bronzy pink in winter, ht 45cm, sp 60cm (18 × 24in); and 'Dart's Blanket', ht 30cm, sp 180cm (12 × 72in), resistant to salt spray, with reddish-purple leaves in autumn. Any well-drained soil, including chalk; full sun, dry or damp, light shade. No pruning.

Euonymus 'Emerald 'n' Gold'

Gaultheria
Evergreen. Two tough, drought-resistant species are rampant *G. shallon,* with rounded, dark green leaves and pink bells in summer, 2m (7ft) and spreading widely by means of underground stems; and *G. procumbens,* a prostrate charmer with small, rounded, glossy evergreen leaves, and white urn-shaped flowers, ht 10cm, sp 100cm (4 × 40in). Light shade; lime-free, moist, peaty or sandy soil.

Genista
Deciduous but appearing evergreen because of close-packed greenish stems, *G. hispanica* (Spanish gorse) is massed with golden pea flowers that light up a cushion of spiny shoots in late spring; ht 60cm, sp 60cm (24 × 24in). Carpeting *G. pilosa,* forming a grey-green carpet, ht 20cm, sp 80cm (8 × 32in) has sprays of yellow flowers also in spring. Ordinary soil, full sun. Hard prune *G. hispanica* when old and straggly to encourage new growth to spring from the base.

Heathers

A generic term to cover hummocky or carpeting winter to spring-flowering *Erica carnea*; late autumn to spring *E.* × *darleyensis*; mid-summer *E. cinerea*, late summer *E. vagans* and *Calluna vulgaris*, and early to late summer *Daboecia cantabrica*. Winter-flowering *Erica carnea* varieties, such as purple-pink 'December Red', 'Springwood Pink' or 'Springwood White', tolerate a little lime; callunas such as double shell-pink 'County Wicklow' and other summer-flowering kinds must have an acid patch.

Some, such as *Erica carnea* 'Foxhollow' and *Calluna vulgaris* 'Golden Carpet', are more valued for their striking, golden-yellow foliage, cheerful on a winter's day, than the blooms they bear. Ht 15-80cm (6-32in). Sp 50-180cm (20-84in). Many root as they spread to form dense, weed-stifling carpets. Plant in sun or light shade.

Hebe pinguifolia 'Pagei'

Hebe

An evergreen, also called shrubby veronica, most species are frost hardy. A reliable, slow-growing mat former is *H. pinguifolia* 'Pagei', ht 30cm, sp 80cm (12 × 32in), and prized for its tiny, elliptic steel-blue leaves on stems clad with spikes of small summer-white flowers. Equally keen to please is *H. pimeloides* 'Quicksilver', ht 30cm, sp 50cm (12 × 20in), with wiry blackish shoots sleeved with silver-blue leaves. Ordinary, well-drained soil in full sun or light shade.

Hypericum calycinum

Large, golden, shaving-brush blooms peeping from a thick carpet of smooth, bright green leaves characterise this eager little mat former, ht 30cm, sp 90cm (12 × 36in), which roots wherever its stems touch the ground. Ordinary, well-drained soil, including chalk: full sun to dense shade. It carpets well beneath conifers. Trim overgrown patches hard back as this will encourage dense new growth.

Hypericum calycinum

Lonicera pileata

Forms a symmetrically stunning hummock of horizontal stems decked with box-like evergreen leaves; tiny purple berries in late summer; shoots root as they spread. Any well-drained soil; sun or shade. Ht 60cm. Sp 120cm (2 × 4ft). No maintenance.

Mahonia aquifolium

(Oregon grape or holly-leaved berberis) Sprays of scented yellow flowers in spring. Fast-spreading suckering shoots form thicket of shining, deeply divided evergreen leaves, fiery tinted in autumn. Choice varieties: 'Apollo', with bronzy green leaves in winter; 'Atropurpurea', with reddish-purple leaves in winter and spring, bloomed, bluish-black berries in autumn. Any well-drained soil, in sun or shade, will suffice. Ht 60cm Sp 120cm (2 × 4ft).

Pachysandra terminalis

Clusters of diamond-shaped evergreen leaves on short stems; tiny, scented, white flowers in late winter. Rampant, ivy-like carpeter with suckering shoots for light, lime-free soil; sun, dense shade. 'Variegata' has bright, white-variegated leaves that light up ground beneath trees and shrubs. Ht 20cm. Sp 40cm (8 × 16in).

Pernettya mucronata

Brilliant clusters of polished white, pink, red and crimson berries on wiry stems sheathed with small dark evergreen leaves. 'Bell's Seedling' is self-fertile with large red berries. Others, such as pink berried 'Lilian', need pollen to set the fruit. Plant one male to three females. Prefers moist, humus-rich, lime-free soil. Best in sun, tolerates light shade. Trim leggy plants in spring. Ht 90cm (3ft). Sp indefinite.

Mahonia aquifolium bears its fragrant flowers in March and April

33

Potentilla fruticosa

Twiggy, deciduous, with small, silky-haired, finely divided leaves; buttercup-like flowers throughout summer. Moist, well-drained soil, sun or light shade. Several varieties, but exceptional carpeters are 'Elizabeth' with primrose-yellow flowers, ht 90cm, sp 120cm (3 × 4ft), and *mandschurica*, silvery leaves, white flowers, ht 30cm, sp 80cm (12 × 32in). Hard-prune young plants in spring.

Prunus laurocerasus

Bushy 'Otto Luyken' and low and spreading 'Zabeliana', both with shining, willow-like evergreen leaves and spikes of white 'candle' blooms in spring, are reliable carpeting cousins of common laurel. Any well-drained soil; sun to deep shade. Ht 1.2m. Sp 1.8m (4 × 6ft).

Silvery *Salix lanata*

Roses

A new breed of sprawling, ground-hugging and repeat-flowering roses pioneered by Mattocks Roses of Oxford include ferny-leaved 'Snow Carpet', double white flowers, June to October, ht 15cm, sp 80cm (6 × 32in); 'Red Blanket', semi-double rose-red, disease-resistant, with leaves retained well into winter, ht 80cm, sp 1.5m (32 × 60in); and 'The Fairy', double coral-pink, ht 70cm, sp 1.2m (2 × 4ft). Thrive in poor soil, sun or light shade.

Rosmarinus lavandulaceus

Clusters of tiny, pale lavender flowers form freely in late spring on dense, mat-forming, rooting stems clad with strongly aromatic leaves. Good for stabilizing steep banks. Slow spreader. Drought resister for light, sandy soils in full sun. Hardy in warm, seaside gardens. Ht 30cm. Sp 1.2m (1 × 4ft).

Prunus laurocerasus 'Otto Luyken'

Rubus calycinoides

Handsome, puckered, three- to five-lobed dark green leaves crowd sinuous, ever-eager stems that root as they rapidly spread, to form a dense evergreen mat. Insignificant white summer flowers are followed by scarlet fruits concealed by a leaf canopy. Any well drained soil, sun or shade. Ideal for colonizing steep slopes or extensive patches beneath trees. Ht 60cm (2ft). Sp indefinite.

Salix

Two weed-smothering species are the woolly willow (*Salix lanata*), whose rounded silvery leaves on prostrate stems complement a profusion of erect yellowish-grey, woolly catkins in spring, and *S. repens argentea*, prized for its silvery leaves which follow spring yellow catkins. Both enjoy moist or boggy soil; the latter favouring wet, coastal sandy patches; sun or light shade. Ht 30cm. Sp 1.2m (1 × 4ft).

Salvia officinalis

Cheerful rooting mat of handsome woolly leaves, purplish grey-green in 'Purpurascens' and variegated yellowish-white and grey-green in 'Icterina'; sparse, lavender-blue flowers in summer. Good front of border plant. Cut back frosted shoots in late spring. Best in light, well-drained soil in full sun. Ht 60cm. Sp 80cm (24 × 32in).

Santolina

Aptly named cotton lavender, with soft or lemon yellow, button-like flowers in summer. Dense, spreading hummocks of evergreen aromatic, feathery foliage. *S. chamaecyparissus* is a white form, ht 45cm, sp 80cm (18 × 32in). Even more snowy is *S. neapolitana*, ht 80cm, sp 120cm (32 × 120in). Any light, well-drained soil, full sun.

Symphoricarpos

(Snowberry) Dense and sprawling 'Hancock', weed stifler supreme, develops a rapid-rooting thicket of small, rounded leaves. Tiny white summer flowers followed by pink berries in autumn. Taller varieties make good wind breaks; sun or shade; ideal under trees; tolerates drips from branches. Well-drained soil. Ht 60cm. Sp 2m (2 × 6ft).

Viburnum davidii

Spreading hummock of leathery, elliptic and quilted evergreen leaves. Male and female flowers borne on separate plants. Clusters of summer white flowers followed, on females, by small turquoise-blue berries. Plant in groups of three females to one male for a good display. Sun or light shade; any well-drained soil, including chalk. Ht 80cm. Sp 1.5cm (32 × 60in).

Vinca

(Periwinkle) Rampant evergreen spring-flowering carpeter with rounded or oval pointed green, golden or silver-variegated leaves, rooting as it spreads. Two commonly grown species are vigorous *V. major*, ht 40cm (16in), sp indefinite, and less invasive and preferred *V. minor*, ht 20cm (8in), sp indefinite. Sun or shade, acid or chalky soil.

Vinca minor 'Variegata'

CONIFERS

Chamaecyparis lawsoniana 'Rijnhof'

Evergreen. Fetching filigree of fresh green ferny leaves spreads slowly to form an overlapping carpet. Sun or light shade; any drained soil. Ht 15cm. Sp 1.5m (6 × 60in).

Juniperus horizontalis

Evergreen. Aptly called the creeping juniper. Eager-to-carpet varieties with feathery, steel-blue foliage are 'Banff'; 'Blue Chip', whose leaves turn bluish-grey in winter; and 'Glauca'. All associate well with heathers and bushy conifers. No maintenance apart from cutting back intruding shoots. Any well-drained soil, full sun or light shade. Ht 15cm sp 150cm (6 × 60in).

Taxus baccata

Evergreen. Hummocky yews to keep down weeds are 'Dovastanii Aurea Pendula', its wide-spreading, pendulous branches clad with variegated golden-yellow foliage, ht 90cm, sp 120cm (3 × 4ft); 'Repens Aurea', a prostrate gem with golden leaves, ht 40cm, sp 120cm (1¼ × 4ft) and 'Summergold', semi-prostrate, bright golden-yellow, ht 40cm, sp 1.5m (1½ × 5ft). Sun or shade, any well-drained soil; ideal for chalk.

CLIMBERS

Many are as adept at carpeting – producing mounds of bright blossom and sculpted leaves.

Clematis armandii

Fast-sprawling evergreen with handsome, pointed and shining trifoliate leaves, on sinuous stems. Vanilla-scented white flowers in spring; ideal for carpeting steep banks. Ht 30cm. Sp 7.2m (1 × 24ft).

Lathyrus latifolia

Needs a warm, sheltered position; any humus-rich soil – including chalk – that stays cool and moist in the summer months.

Hedera

(Ivy) What a rampageous, shade-tolerant, prostrate family! Rooting as it spreads. Choose from *H. helix*, variegated silver-grey 'Glacier', lacy 'Ivalace', or 'Pin Oak', with a curiously long terminal lobe to its leaf. *H. colchica* 'Dentata Variegata' has enormous dark green leaves suffused with gold; and, in 'Paddy's Pride', each leaf has a central butter-yellow blotch. Any soil is suitable, apart from soggy patches. Sun to dense shade. Ht 15cm. Sp 3.6m (6 × 144in).

Hydrangea petiolaris

Fresh, green, heart-shaped leaves deck stems – in well-established plants – tipped with a summer show of 15cm (6in) cartwheel blooms of delicate, lacy white and green flowers. Any well-drained soil, in sun or light shade. Ideal for brightening dull, chilly spots. Ht 45cm. Sp 3.6m (1½ × 12ft). No maintenance.

Lathyrus latifolius

(Everlasting pea) An herbaceous rapid romper with slender shoots clothed in summer with long-stemmed sweet pea blooms in magenta-pink, pale pink or white. Revels in full sun and humusy well-drained soil. 'White Pearl' is a winsome sprawler that will grow well on a sunny terrace, patio or dry slope. Ht 30cm. Sp 1.8m (1 × 6ft).

Lonicera

(Honeysuckle) Fragrant, with small clusters of biscuit-yellow blooms in summer, the evergreen form, L. japonica 'Halliana', makes a wide spreading carpet of broad, deep green leaves. Ht 30cm. Sp 1.8m (1 × 6ft). Also richly scented and thickly sprawling are its leaf-shedding cousins L. periclymenum 'Belgica' (Early Dutch), with rounded heads of pale rose-purple, yellow-lipped blooms, and deeper hued L. p. 'Serotina' (Late Dutch) which, between them, are miracles of colour from early to late summer. Any well-drained, fertile soil, sun or light shade. Ht 30cm. Sp 1.5m (1 × 5ft).

Parthenocissus

We expect ivy-leaved Virginia creeper (P. quinquefolia) and the small, pointed, three-lobed leaves of P. tricuspidata 'Veitchii' to brighten a wall with fiery autumn-tinted leaves, but it comes as a pleasant surprise to find them flamboyantly colonizing and colouring a bank or edge of a patio or terrace. Any well-drained soil will suffice, either in sun or light shade. Ht 30cm. Sp 3m (1 × 9ft).

HERBACEOUS PLANTS

Acanthus

(Bear's breeches) A noble, statuesque drought resister. There are two species: A. mollis latifolus, with a rosette of dark shining green and broadly lobed leaves, and A. spinosus, similar, but with jaggedly cut foliage. In summer, each sports a 1.2m (4ft) spike of cowled mauve and white flowers. Any well-drained soil. Sun or shade. Needs winter protection in cold districts. Ht 80cm. Sp 90cm (32 × 36in).

Alchemilla mollis

(Lady's mantle) Uncomplaining in hot droughty spells, its appealing rosettes of rounded, softly hairy, pale green leaves – rain drops can be rolled upon them – and summer sprays of starry, greenish-yellow blooms, are beloved by flower arrangers. Thrives in any well-drained soil; full sun or light shade. Ht 30cm. Sp 60cm (12 × 24in).

Parthenocissus tricuspidata

Anaphalis triplinervis
(Pearly everlasting) Suckering, whitish-grey, felted long to oval leaves; stems topped with papery whitish flowers in late summer. Shows no sign of discomfort in parched ground. Rampant; for hot banks and beside hedges. Any soil, sun or very light shade. Ht 20cm. Sp 60cm (8 × 24in).

Artemisia stelleriana
Filigree of deeply fingered grey-white, ground-hugging leaves; small yellow flowers in summer, providing an excellent foil for other perennials. A rapid clump-forming sprawler, it thrives in seaside gardens. Any well-drained soil, full sun. Ht 25cm. Sp 90cm (10 × 36in).

Aruncus sylvester
Vertically thrusting clump of ferny-leaved stems topped with arching, plumy sprays of small creamy flowers in early summer. Dense; spreads slowly. Luxuriant in deep, moist, well-drained soil; less robust but equally appealing in light, sandy patches. Plants arc of separate sexes; males have the finest plumes. Ht 1.5m. Sp 1.8m (5 × 6ft).

Artemisia stelleriana

Asperula odorata
(Sweet woodruff) Greatly under-rated weed-proof colonizer; rampageous. Stems of whorled green leaves topped with fragrant, starry white flowers in late spring. Well-drained soil, specially chalk. Light or dense shade. Spreads by underground runners. Good for planting in the excessively dry areas beneath trees and shrubs. Ht 12.5cm. Sp 1m (5 × 36in).

Astilbe × arendsii
Green or bronzy-red, ferny-leaved clump former with feathery flowers in plumy spikes. Rich pink 'Bressingham Beauty', pure white 'Bridal Veil', dark crimson 'Fanal', salmon-red 'Fire', rosy purple A. tacquetii 'Superba' colour summer. Moist soil; sun or light shade for this elegant waterside plant. Ht 50cm. Sp 45cm (20 × 18in).

Astrantia
(Masterwort) Shaggy, green-tinged white flowers in A. major, with handsome, deeply-lobed, mottled cream and yellow leaves in its variety 'Variegata'. A. rubra has crimson blooms. Both brighten mid summer. Well-drained soil; sun or light shade. Beloved by flower arrangers. Ht 60cm. Sp 45cm (24 × 18in).

Bergenia
(Elephant's ear) Large, rounded, leathery, evergreen and densely carpeting leaves; thick-stemmed sprays of tubular fleshy flowers in early spring. Choice hybrids: rosy-red 'Abendglut', 'Silberlicht', white, reddish-pink 'Sunningdale'. The foliage of mauve-carmine B. cordifolia 'Purpurea' assumes glowing purplish tints in winter. Moist, well-drained soil; sun or shade. Ht 30cm. Sp 45cm (12 × 18in).

Bergenia 'Silberlicht'

Brunnera macrophylla

Resembles a giant forget-me-not with large, hairy, heart-shaped leaves; innumerable peeping blue flowers in spring. Less vigorous 'Variegata' has primrose-variegated leaves that contrast effectively with its sky-blue blossom. Fast, suckering spreader for cool, moist soil in light or dense shade. Dislikes being planted in dry spots. Ht 40cm. Sp 120cm (16 × 48in).

Cerastium tomentosum

(Snow-in-summer) Invasive carpeter valued for its cheering mat of small, silver-grey leaves and white, pink-like flowers in early summer. Full sun or dappled shade; well-drained soil. Ht 22.5cm. Sp 90cm (9 × 36in).

Convallaria majalis

Statuesque canopy of pointed, glossy leaves interspersed with sprays of waxy white, richly scented, bell-shaped flowers in spring; 'Fortin's Giant' has large impressive blooms, while less vigorous 'Rosea' is acclaimed for its pinkish-white flowers. Spreads quickly by underground runners. Prefers cool, shady spots in well-drained, humus-rich soil, including chalk. Ht 45cm. Sp 60cm (9 × 24in).

Cornus canadensis

Cornus canadensis

Slow mover with underground shoots that form a carpet of rosettes – each a cluster of four, rounded green leaves and, in spring, set with an exquisite four-petalled white flower. Perfect for underplanting azaleas, rhododendrons and pine trees. Needs a peaty, acid soil; light or deep shade. Ht 15cm. Sp 60cm (6 × 24in).

Crocosmia

Impressive grassy or sword-leaved, corm-rooted plant with dense or loosely-spaced sprays of flared lily-like blooms in late summer. Spreads rapidly to form a dense upthrusting clump. Choice varieties: 'Citronella', with soft creamy flowers; deep orange, crimson-throated 'Emily McKenzie'. The Bressingham hybrids have broader, stiffer leaves and larger flowers. Distinctive are orange-red 'Emberglow', orange-flame 'Bressingham Blaze' and 'Lucifer'. Any light, fertile, well-drained soil in sun or shade. Ht 60-75cm. Sp 90cm (24-30 × 36in).

Dianthus

(Garden pinks) Spreading quickly to form a mat of bluish evergreen leaves, richly clove-scented Old World garden pinks, such as fringed rose-pink 'Earl of Essex', blush-mauve 'Freda', shell-pink 'Inchmery', double white 'Mrs Sinkins' and 'White Ladies' are superb for edging beds and borders, or colouring crazy paving. Any well-drained, humus-rich, preferably limy soil; full sun. Ht 15cm. Sp 45cm (6 × 18in).

Dicentra

(Ladies' lockets) Fine weed stiflers producing wide, ferny hummocks are *D. formosa*, with pink-hued stems and mauve-pink heart-shaped lockets, ice-white in its 'Alba' form, from early to late spring; and top-value *D. eximea* 'Luxuriant', which sports a fine succession of showy, bright red lockets throughout summer. Best in light, lime-free soil in shade or full shade. Ht 30cm. Sp 90cm (12 × 36in).

Doronicum caucasicum

(Leopard's bane) Rapid clump former, with slender-stemmed yellow daisies in spring; deep green, heart-shaped leaves. Single flowered 'Miss Mason', double flowered 'Spring Beauty' and single 'Magnificum' flourish in sun or light shade. Any soil; must be cool, moist and humus rich, otherwise leaves rapidly wilt. Ht 45-60cm. Sp 60cm (18-24 × 24in).

Epimedium

Fast spreader with creeping roots. Almost evergreen, marbled, three-lobed leaves on wiry stems, and exquisite, miniature columbine flowers in several pastel shades. Ideal for woodland shade and under-planting trees and shrubs. Choice species are pale yellow *E. versicolor* 'Sulphureum', deep pink *E. macran-* *thum* 'Roseum' and bronzy-yellow *E. perralderianum*. Well-drained soil; sun or deep shade. Ht 30cm. Sp 45cm (12 × 18in).

Euphorbia

(Spurge) Handsome, suckering thicket-former with flower-like bracts. *E. griffithii* 'Fireglow' has long leaves clustering the stem and bright, flame-coloured blooms; *E.g.* 'Great Dixter' is a darker-leaved form. *E. robbiae* is quite different, with greenish-yellow flowers thrusting from rosettes of long, leathery round-tipped leaves. Both thrive in sun or deep shade. Any well-drained soil. Ht 60cm. Sp 80cm (24 × 32in).

Helleborus orientalis, purple form

Geranium

(Cranesbill) Colourful and adaptable family of rapid trailing, rooting spreaders and tussock formers with rounded, usually deeply-cut leaves. Invaluable carpeters are *Geranium endressii* 'Wargrave Pink', with silvery pink flowers, ht 80cm (32in), sp 120cm (4ft); *G. macrorrhizum* with aromatic leaves, white-flowered in 'Album', magenta in 'Bevan's Variety' and pale lilac in 'Ingwersen's Variety', ht 30cm (12in), sp 90cm (36in). Also recommended are magenta-purple *G. sanguineum* and its white 'Album' form. Any well-drained soil; either in sun or shade.

Lamium maculatum 'Beacon Silver'

Helleborus
Architectural clumpish carpeter. *H. foetidus* has sculpted, deeply divided evergreen leaves and nodding heads of green-belled, maroon-rimmed flowers in late winter; *H. corsicus* is prized for its coarsely toothed tri-lobed leaves and open, apple-green flowers in early spring. *H. orientalis* (Lenten rose) has divided, almost evergreen leaves, and sprays of white to plum-purple flowers in late winter and spring. All thrive in well-drained heavy or light soil, including chalk. Sun to deep shade. Ht 30-60cm. Sp 60cm (12-24 × 24in).

Hemerocallis
(Day lily) Slow-spreading clumps of long grassy leaves decked with thin-stemmed, lily-like flowers in summer. Spectacular hybrids are cherry-red, greenish-yellow throated 'Alan', clear yellow 'Dorothy McDade', terracotta suffused with gold 'Lochinvar' and true pink 'Pink Damask'. Full sun or light shade. Ht 60-80cm. Sp 60-80cm (24-32 × 24-32in).

Heuchera
Enchanting close-knit carpeter for border edges, with flat, rounded, hairy and marbled leaves; froth of tiny bell-shaped flowers in early summer. Look for greenish-white 'Greenfinch', coral-red 'Coral Cloud' and scarlet 'Shere Variety'. 'Palace Purple' is arrestingly different with deep purple leaves and white flowers. Well drained light or heavy soil. Sun or light shade. Ht 30-90cm. Sp 45cm (12-36in × 18in).

Hosta
(Plantain lily) Probably our most versatile ground-cover plant. Many new Japanese varieties are swelling an already wide range of strikingly hued leaves. Beloved by flower arrangers also for its decorative geometric rosettes. Arresting indeed are *H. sieboldiana (glauca)* with immense, quilted bluish-grey leaves and pale lilac-white flowers; *H. fortunei*, greenish-blue leaves and lilac blooms, and 'Aureo-Picta', with butter-yellow-edged, green leaves, later turning soft green and olive. Any soil, from parched to soggy; full sun to dense shade. Ht 25-75cm. Sp 30-60cm (10-32 × 12-24in).

Iris foetidissima
Handsome thrusting tuft of narrow, deep green leathery leaves and exquisite pale biscuit-yellow flowers in early summer. Full sun, but ideal for colonizing shady spots under trees or around buildings. Any soil; but grows best on chalk. Ht 45cm. Sp 60cm (18 × 24in).

Lamium maculatum
Good non-invasive, spring-flowering carpeters are 'Beacon Silver', with green-rimmed, silver leaves and pink dead nettle flowers; 'Shell-Pink', with frosted green and white foliage; and 'White Nancy', bright with exceptionally silvered leaves and ivory white blooms. Sun or light shade; any well-drained soil. Ht 15cm. Sp 90cm (6 × 36in).

Liriope muscari

Bright grape hyacinth-like spikes of lilac-blue bells on short stems amid a rosette of grassy leaves, from mid summer to early autumn. Sun or very light shade; ordinary, well-drained light or heavy soil; resists droughty spells. Ht 30cm. Sp 45cm (12 × 18in).

Lysimachia

(Loosestrife) Upright, clump-forming, pointed-leaved *L. punctata*, with spikes of canary-yellow flowers, ht 75cm, sp 90cm (30 × 36in), and carpeting, rooting, new-penny golden-leaved *L. nummularia* 'Aurea', ht 7cm, sp 60cm (3 × 24in) thrive in heavy or light soils. Both flower in mid summer and enjoy moist conditions; sun or light shade.

Polygonum affine 'Superbum'

Meconopsis betonicifolia

(Blue Himalayan poppy) Arresting clumps of sky-blue, yellow-centred blooms in early summer; sturdy stems clad with narrow, light green, hairy leaves. Fastidious; needs humus-rich, lime-free soil and cool, dappled shade. Spreads slowly. Ht 90cm. Sp 90cm (36 × 36in).

Physalis franchetii

(Chinese lantern, cape gooseberry) Summer white flowers top thick stems sheathed with rounded, hairy leaves; each orange-scarlet pod is filled with an orange berry. Valued for dried arrangements. Rapid spreader with invasive roots. Ordinary well-drained soil; sun or shade. Ht 75cm. Sp 120cm (30 × 48in).

Polygonatum multiflorum

(Solomon's seal) Elegant arching stems set with serried rows of hanging waxy, whitish-green, tube-like flowers in spring; broad, pointed leaves. Suckering spreader for cool, well-drained soil, including chalk.

Sun to deep shade. Ht 80cm. Sp 90cm (32 × 36in).

Polygonum

(Knotweed) Inelegant name for the imposing *Polygonum bistorta* 'Superbum', bright with pink, poker-like blooms from late spring to summer; thick canopy of large, dock-like leaves. Ht 90cm. Sp 120cm (36 × 48in). Its small, thickly carpeting cousin, *P. affine* 'Darjeeling Red', roots as it spreads and sports shoals of small leaves and deep pink pokers from mid to late summer. Ht 25cm. Sp 90cm (10 × 36in). Cool, moist soil, sun or light shade.

Prunella webbiana

Prized for its rampant mat of ground-hugging, rounded leaves and summer spikes of dead-nettle flowers, pinkish-red in 'Little Red Riding Hood', and lilac in 'Loveliness'. Full sun or light shade. Definitely prefers well-drained, humus-rich soil. Ht 20cm. Sp 60cm (8 × 24in). Self-seeds if not dead-headed regularly.

Pulmonaria
(Lungwort) Woodlander with wide spreading rosettes of long, broad, pointed leaves, silvery white in *P. saccharata* 'Argentea', with small, tubular clusters of pink-budded blue flowers in late winter; and mottled green and white in 'Bowles' Red', with red blooms. *P. angustifolia* 'Mawson's Variety' is a charming departure, with tall sprays of gentian-blue flowers borne above rich green leaves. Moist, well-drained soil, sun or light shade. Ht 30cm. Sp 60cm (12 × 24in).

Rodgersia
Statuesque clump former; huge, ground-shading leaves in *R. tabularis*, with clusters of starry white flowers in late summer; five-fingered, triangular and copper-tinted leaves in *R. podophylla*, with plumy heads of creamy astilbe-like flowers. Both thrive in cool, moist or marshy soil. Good waterside plants. Ht 60-90cm. Sp 90-120cm (2-3 × 3-4ft).

Sedum spectabile
(Ice plant) Dense clump former. Large platform blooms from summer to autumn attract tortoiseshell butterflies. 'Brilliant' bears glistening pink flowers and fleshy, rounded blue-green leaves; 'Autumn Joy', has blooms that are coppery pink. Well-drained, humus-rich soil, sun or very light shade. Ht 40-60cm. Sp 60-75cm (16-24 × 24-30in).

Stachys byzantina
(Lamb's ears) Long, woolly and silvery leaves sprawl and mat the surface; foraging stems root freely. Spikes of silver and mauve flowers in summer. Well-drained light or heavy soil, full sun. Ht 45cm. Sp 90cm (18 × 36in). A non-flowering cousin is *S. lanata* 'Silver Carpet'. Ht 15cm. Sp 90cm (6 × 36in).

Symphytum
(Comfrey) Rooting sprawl of large, broad, hairy leaves foil sprays of tubular flowers in spring: creamy white in *Symphytum grandiflorum* and bluish-pink in 'Hidcote'. 'Variegatum' has creamy-yellow-edged leaves to light up shady spots. Cool, moist, well-drained soil; sun to full shade. Ht 15-25cm. Sp 60-90cm (6-10 × 24-36in).

Tellima grandiflora
Exquisite clump former with rounded hairy leaves, coppery in winter; small creamy bells on slender, erect stems in late spring. 'Purpurea' is an attractive variety with purplish leaves and pink bells. Porous, humus-rich soil; sun or light shade. Ht 45cm. Sp 60-90cm (18 × 24-36in).

Trachystemon orientale
Rapid spreader with large hairy, crimpled green leaves that prettily overlap; blue flowers in spring. Thrives in poor sandy or heavy clay soil. Good under large shrubs; sun to dense shade. Very adaptable. Ht 60cm. Sp 90cm (24 × 36in).

Tellima grandiflora

ROCK PLANTS

Acaena
Prostrate carpeter forming a dense filigree of finely divided leaves, blue-grey with red stems in *A. affinis;* soft pewter-blue in *A. sanguisorbe.* Good paving cover and a perfect foil for small flowering plants. Well-drained soil, full sun. Ht 5-10cm. Sp 60cm (2-4 × 24in).

Ajuga
(Bugle) Rosette-forming ground hugger, rooting as it spreads; small rounded leaves. *Ajuga reptans'* varieties include 'Alba', with crinkly, bronze-tinted green leaves and spikes of white-lipped flowers in spring. 'Burgundy Glow' has suffused rose, cream and magenta leaves, blue flowers; 'Multicolour' has bronze, pink and cream leaves; and 'Purpurea' has blue flowers that contrast well with burnished purple foliage. Moist, well-drained soil, sun or light shade. Ht 10cm. Sp 60cm (4 × 24in).

Alyssum saxatile
Broad, sprawling hummock of small, grey-green leaves decked, in spring, with cool lemon flowers in 'Citrinum', long-lasting double flowers in 'Plenum' and apricot blooms in 'Dudley Neville'. Well-drained soil and a site in full sun. Ht 25cm. Sp 45cm (10 × 18in).

Anthemis nobilis (Chamaemelum)
(Chamomile) Carpeting, rooting filigree of ferny green leaves. Non-flowering 'Treneague' makes a fine ornamental lawn; 'Flore-Pleno' is a double-flowered variety with exquisite white pom-pon blooms in mid-summer. Transforms rock garden pockets. Best grown in full sun and a light, porous soil. Ht 10cm. Sp 60cm (4 × 24in).

Ajuga reptans 'Burgundy Glow'

Aubrieta deltoidea
Dense tiny-leaved sprawler, aglow with small richly coloured flowers in early spring. Choice varieties include double carmine 'Alex Brett', double reddish-purple 'Bob Saunders', double-flowered 'Bressingham Pink', deep violet 'Dr Mules' and rich bluish 'Triumphant'. 'Aurea Variegata' forms a greenish golden-variegated mat starred in spring with lavender flowers. Thrives in any well-drained patch, but prefers limy soil; full sun. Ht 10-20cm. Sp 60cm (4-8 × 24in).

Campanula
(Bell flower) Intrusive spreader with questing stems set with small, deep green leaves and innumerable sprays of starry flowers in summer; deep blue in rampant *C. portenschlagiana* (*muralis*) and sky-blue flowers in less invasive 'Stella'. Sun or very light shade; well-drained soil. Ht 10cm. Sp 60cm (4 × 24in).

44

Dryas octopetala
(Mountain avens) Evergreen with ground-hugging, rounded leaves, large, white, cup-shaped flowers in spring and summer; arresting feathery seed clusters. Any, well-drained soil, sun or light shade. Ht 10-15cm. Sp 60cm (4 × 24in).

Helianthemum
(Sun rose) Accommodating, weed-proof sprawler with neat evergreen leaves; stems studded with tiny saucer-shaped flowers from late spring to mid summer. Choice garden hybrids include coppery-salmon 'Ben Dearg', crimson 'Firefly', soft pink 'Wisley Pink' and very large and stunning yellow 'Wisley Primrose'. Best in porous soil, full sun. Ht 15cm. Sp 70cm (6 × 30in).

Lithospermum diffusum
Sprawling evergreen of great beauty. Sinuous stems clad with small leaves; tiny, flared caerulean-blue trumpet blooms from late spring to summer. Needs a humus-rich, lime-free soil; full sun or very light shade. Ht 20cm. Sp 90cm (8 × 36in).

Omphalodes verna
(Blue-eyed Mary) Tight, creeping mat of broadly oval leaves; stems almost hidden beneath a mantle of sapphire-blue flowers in spring. Cool, deep, leafy soil; sun or light shade. Ht 10cm. Sp 60cm (4 × 24in).

Phlox
Breathtaking flower-decked drapes are yours for planting small-leaved *Phlox douglasii*, with starry pink, white or blue flowers; the hybrid *P.* × 'Millstream' with rich lilac-pink blooms; *P. subulata* 'Temiscaming' with bright cerise flowers. *P. s.* 'Blue Ridge', has lilac-blue, orange-eyed blooms. Needs fertile, well-drained,

Dryas octopetala

humus-rich soil; sun or very light shade. Ht 7.5cm. Sp 90cm (3 × 36in). Trim off spent blooms.

Polygonum vacciniifolium
Mat former that roots as it spreads, with clustered, rich green pointed leaves and erect pink poker blooms valued for a late summer and early autumn display. Sun or deep shade; any well-drained light or heavy soil. Ht 7.5cm. Sp 30cm (3 × 24in).

Saxifraga urbium (umbrosa)
(London pride) Massed rosettes of dark green, rounded leaves foil finely branched sprays of tiny pinkish-white flowers. The soil-hugging mossy saxifrages, such as double pink 'Dartington Double' and blood-red 'Triumph' are colourfully invasive. Cool, well-drained damp spots; sun or light shade. Ht 10cm. Sp 60cm (4 × 24in).

GRASSES

Arundinaria viridistriata
Grassy, tussock-forming bamboo with long, golden-variegated leaves on purplish stems. Intrepid spreader. Well-drained light or heavy soil; sun or shade. Ht 1.2m. Sp 1.8m (4-6ft).

Festuca glauca
Tussocks of rich bluish-green, needle-slender leaves are this grass's claim to fame. Find it a sunny spot in fertile, well-drained soil. Close-set clumps will interweave to form a weed-proof carpet. Ht 25cm. Sp 45cm (9 × 18in).

Luzula maxima
(Woodrush) Excellent carpeter for dry shady spots where other plants shrivel and die. The variety, 'Marginata', bears greenish flowers on slender stems above clumps of broad, white-rimmed, deep green leaves. Light, moist or dry, acid soil. Ht 45cm. Sp 60cm (18-24in).

Milium effusum 'Aureum'
Bowles' golden grass has much to commend it. A natural woodlander, with clumps of broad, golden-yellow leaves – specially bright in spring – illuminating shady spots. Any well-drained soil; sun or partial shade. Ht 35cm. Sp 45cm (14 × 18in).

FERNS

Adiantum pedatum
Once seen, ever remembered. Hardiest of the 'maidenhair' species, it has a creeping rootstock and soft green, finely divided fan-like fronds, tinged red when young. For shady banks where soil is cool, moist and peaty. 'Japonicum' is taller than the species; young fronds tinged pink. Ht 20cm. Sp 60cm (8 × 24in).

Athyrium filix-femina
Enchanting lady fern. Spreads by underground suckers. Very variable, with finely cut fronds. 'Victoriae' has fronds that are an appealing filigree of tasselled crosses. Superb for streamsides or boggy borders. Cool, humus-rich soil, sun or shade. Ht 60cm. Sp 60cm. (24 × 24in).

Blechnum tabulare
Impressive and slightly tender species with long, ladder-like fronds, for sheltered, woodland gardens and other partially shaded spots. Spreads by suckers. Cool, moist, fertile soil enriched with peat or leafmould. Light shade. Ht 90cm. Sp 120cm (36 × 48in).

Fronds of *Blechnum*

Festuca glauca

Spires of *Digitalis purpurea* 'Excelsior Strain'

ANNUALS AND BIENNIALS

Limnanthes douglasii
(Poached egg plant) Annual dense carpeter with fleshy, finely divided leaves and short stems decked with showy summer flowers of half white and half yellow petals. Prolific self-seeder. Full sun, otherwise blooms stay tightly closed; light or well-drained heavy soil. Ht 15cm. Sp 60cm (6 × 24in).

Nasturtium *(Tropaeolum)*
Annual. Rampageous sprawler. Best carpeters are 'Gleam' hybrids with flared trumpet blooms in orange, yellow, red, salmon, cerise and prim-rose borne freely on fleshy stems with rounded shade-casting leaves. Flowers form freely in full sun;

leaves only in light shade. Any soil but not too rich, otherwise an abundance of leaves will be produced at the expense of blossom. Ht 30cm. Sp 60cm (12 × 24in).

Digitalis purpurea
(Foxglove) Biennial or perennial. Breathtaking sight when hillsides are aflame with its spires of deep pinkish-purple blooms from June to August. A woodlander that forms a dense rosette of broad, soft hairy leaves in its first year and a spike of downswept blotched, tubular flowers in its second. The spires of maroon-spotted cream, primrose, pink and purple flowers of *D. purpurea* 'Excelsior Strain', are magnificent. Ht 1.5m. Sp. 45cm (5 × 1½ft). Light shade; deep, humus-rich soil.

INDEX AND ACKNOWLEDGEMENTS

Picture credits

Pat Brindley: 8, 27, 30, 31(b), 32(t,b), 33, 34(t), 35, 46(b), 47.
Derek Gould: 1, 12, 25, 39(1), 42.
ICI: 18(t,b), 19(t,b).
Harry Smith Collection: 4/5, 7(t,b), 9(b), 10(t,b), 11, 14, 20, 21(t,b), 23, 24, 26, 28/9, 31(t), 34(b), 36, 37, 38, 39(r), 40, 41, 43, 44, 46(t).
Michael Warren: 6, 9(t), 13, 15, 22, 45.

Artwork by Simon Roulstone

48